YOUR KNOWLEDGE HAS VALUE

Adam Balogh

EU Socio-Economic Governance

In how far is the OMC an effective tool for European social governance?

GRIN Verlag

Bibliografische Information der Deutschen Nationalbibliothek:

Die Deutsche Bibliothek verzeichnet diese Publikation in der Deutschen National-
bibliografie; detaillierte bibliografische Daten sind im Internet über http://dnb.d-
nb.de/ abrufbar.

Imprint:

Copyright © 2013 GRIN Verlag GmbH
Druck und Bindung: Books on Demand GmbH, Norderstedt Germany
ISBN: 978-3-656-37158-8

This book at GRIN:

http://www.grin.com/en/e-book/209227/eu-socio-economic-governance

GRIN - Your knowledge has value

Der GRIN Verlag publiziert seit 1998 wissenschaftliche Arbeiten von Studenten, Hochschullehrern und anderen Akademikern als eBook und gedrucktes Buch. Die Verlagswebsite www.grin.com ist die ideale Plattform zur Veröffentlichung von Hausarbeiten, Abschlussarbeiten, wissenschaftlichen Aufsätzen, Dissertationen und Fachbüchern.

Visit us on the internet:

http://www.grin.com/

http://www.facebook.com/grincom

http://www.twitter.com/grin_com

CENTRAL EUROPEAN UNIVERSITY

EU Socio-Economic Governance

In how far is the OMC an effective tool for European social

governance?

Adam Balogh

06/01/2013

Contents

1

1. Introduction

In the mid- 1990s, welfare states in Europe were under acute strain. Unemployment had risen dramatically (Trubek/Mosher 2001, 6) and in 1997, 18 per cent of the population of the European Union (EU) lived in a household below the relative income poverty threshold[1] (Armstrong 2010, 1). Although social policies were traditionally tasks of the nation-states, an increasing "Europeanization" of "social exclusion"[2] and the inability of the member states to act in an increasing multi-level governance context led to the need for actions on a European level (Armstrong 2010, 2).

The start was made with the "European Employment Strategy" (EES) (Trubek/Mosher 2001, 6), which became, due to its success, (Trubek/Trubek 2005, 349-351) the forerunner of the "Open Method of Coordination" (OMC) (Sabel/Zeitlin 2008, 289). The OMC, like the EES, is an Instrument of governance in the EU, which is based on voluntary cooperation and rests on soft law mechanism (Borrás/Jacobsson 2004, 189). Armstrong describes the function of the OMC in his Book about European policy coordination as follows: *"The function of the OMC is not to make policy itself but rather to provide a framework within which states are encouraged to identify policy problems and to seek solutions either within their own domestic systems or by learning from the experience of others"* (Armstrong 2010, 9). The reason for this soft law solution was the lack of political support for further transfers of

---

[1] "Households with less than 60% of national equivalized median income." (Armstrong 2010, 1).

[2] The term „social exclusion" is a politically correct circumscription of poverty (Armstrong 2010, 19).

legal competencies to the EU in social areas (Borrás/Jacobsson 2004, 190). But precisely because of this soft law nature, many critics accuse that the OMC is ineffective and even dangerous for further European integration (Trubek/Trubek 2005, 344, 351, 355).

Therefore, the purpose of this term paper is to find an answer to the question: *"In how far is the OMC an effective tool for European social governance?"* and to show whether the OMC is as effective as many European institutions and scholars claim, or just a paper tiger. In order to answer these questions the procedure is as follows: First, a very brief summary of the history and emergence of the OMC, followed by a summary of its principles and impacts. Secondly, a detailed evaluation of the OMC, where also will be shown why it is difficult to evaluate the OMC (and soft laws in general). And thirdly a policy recommendation that considers the discussed evaluation of the OMC.

The answer to the research question plays a very important role because of increasing unemployment and poverty in EU since the European sovereign debt crisis (Süddeutsche.de 2013). If an evaluation of the OMC shows that it is ineffective, maybe the EU should use other policies to overcome current socioeconomic problems.

2. The Open Method of Coordination

The OMC has two forerunners, the Broad Economic Policy Guidelines (BEPG) introduced by the Treaty of Maastricht in 1992 (Sabel/Zeitlin 2008, 289) and the more immediate EES, which was formalized in the 1997 Amsterdam treaty (Art. 128 EC) (Armstrong 2010, 33). Due to its success in reforming the labor market in the EU on the one hand (Trubek/Trubek 2005, 349-351) and its methodology, which allows member states to keep their legislative competence in this policy domain, on the other (Armstrong 2010, 33), the principles of the EES were transferred to the OMC later. In 2000, after an Extraordinary European Council meeting in Lisbon, the heads of states admitted a new strategic goal that included a better coordination of national economic policies and that the OMC should become the driving motor (Armstrong 2010, 29 | Borrás/Jacobsson 2004, 187). The main difference between the EES and the OMC is that the first one is a treaty based process, while the OMC process has emerged through institutional practices (Armstrong 2010, 34).

But there are also three deeper reasons that are accountable for the establishment of the OMC: Firstly, strong economic disfunctionalities due to a globalized economy and increased worldwide competition (Borrás/Jacobsson 2004, 186). Secondly, the political consideration to build up a social dimension in the EU, which became possible with these new open methods (Borrás/Jacobsson 2004, 186). And thirdly, a strong crisis in EU legitimacy in the 1990s, where the OMC has been seen as a tool to introduce more democratic ways in decision-making (Borrás/Jacobsson 2004, 186-187).

But what exactly is the OMC and how does it work? As already mentioned in the introduction, the OMC is an Instrument of governance in the EU, which is based on voluntary cooperation and rests on soft law mechanism (Borrás/Jacobsson 2004, 189). Armstrong describes it as follows: *"The function of the OMC is not to make policy itself but rather to provide a framework within which states are encouraged to identify policy problems and to seek solutions either within their own domestic systems or by learning from the experience of others"* (Armstrong 2010, 9). Further he, as Sabel and Zeitlin, describes the OMC as a way of "experimentalist governance" (Armstrong 2010, 15 | Sabel/Zeitlin 2008, 274), which hinders its analysis through the typical variants of "institutionalism" (Armstrong 2010, 12-13).

From a "philosophical" point of view there is a difference between policy coordination in the sense of cooperation and policy coordination as convergence. While cooperation comes together with state autonomy and sanction-free learning, convergence always contains some kind of reduction in policy diversity (Armstrong 2010, 41). Of course the OMC with its sanction-free principles and its focus on mutual learning falls into the philosophy of cooperation.

Another possible classification of the OMC is to distinguish between so called "hard law" and "soft law". While hard law contains strong policy instruments like (top-down) binding instructions and sanction mechanism, the mechanism of soft law work less binding and sanction-free (Borrás/Jacobsson 2004, 195 | Trubek/Mosher 2001, 5). Although scholars agree that the OMC is built upon soft law mechanism (Trubek/Mosher 2001, 5 | Armstrong 2010, 43 | Buchkremer/Zirra 2007, 166), there is a debate going on whether the OMC is ineffective and even dangerous for further European integration (Trubek/Trubek 2005, 344, 351, 355).

A detailed look at the methods of the OMC shows why it is handled as a soft law. Borrás and Jacobsson write about these methods while referring to a European Council Conclusion: *"The main procedures of this method are: common guidelines to be translated into national policy, combined with periodic monitoring, evaluation and peer review organized as mutual learning processes and accompanied by indicators and benchmarks as means of comparing best practice"*. Borrás and Jacobsson also recognize, however, at least seven points that make the OMC different from traditional soft law and the following table shows their results (Borrás/Jacobsson 2004, 188):

Table 1 Differences between the OMC and the traditional soft law	
The open method of co-ordination	The traditional soft law
Intergovernmental approach: the Council and the Commission have a dominant role	Supranational approach: the Commission and the Court of Justice have a dominant role
Political monitoring at the highest level	Administrative monitoring
Clear procedures and iterative process	Weak and ad-hoc procedures
Systematic linking across policy areas	No explicit linking of policy areas
Interlinking EU and national public action	No explicit linking of EU/national levels
Seeks the participation of social actors	Does not explicitly seek participation
Aims at enhancing learning processes	No explicit goal of enhancing learning is stated

(Borrás/Jacobsson 2004, 188)

Therefore, Borrás and Jacobsson came to the conclusion that the OMC is based on following principles: voluntarism, subsidiarity, flexibility, participation, policy integration, and multi-level integration (Borrás/Jacobsson 2004, 189). But how is the EU itself defining the working methods of the OMC? The Portuguese Presidency defined the OMC at the Lisbon Summit as follows (Sabel/Zeitlin 2008, 290-291 | Trubek/Trubek 2005, 348 | Lisbon European Council Presidency Conclusions 2000, §37):

- Fixing guidelines for the Union combined with specific timetables for achieving the goals which they set in the short, medium and long term;

- establishing, where appropriate, quantitative and qualitative indicators and benchmarks against the best in the world and tailored to the needs of different member states and sectors as a means of comparing best practices;

- translating these European guidelines into national and regional policies by setting specific targets and adopting measures, taking into account national and regional differences;

- periodic monitoring, evaluation and peer review organized as mutual learning processes.

Although many scholars agree on a potential usefulness of the OMC, also many find potential problems that might occur. Borrás and Jacobsson identified for example three policy areas where the OMC would only apply under hard efforts, like areas of public involvement, sensitive national political areas and monetary/economic areas (Borrás/Jacobsson 2004, 191). Further they also identify free riding problems due to a lack of sanctions (Borrás/Jacobsson 2004, 196) and possible negative effects on judicial and political accountability due to a dilution of decision-making and implementation (Borrás/Jacobsson 2004, 199). Armstrong also points to a lack of accountability (Armstrong 2010, 51) and warns of the "destabilizing" effect to the domestic area of decision-making by the OMC (Armstrong 2010, 49). Sabel and Zeitlin, however, are concerned about the negative image of EES, which could spill over to OMC. They write: *"Especially in its early years, the EES was widely regarded as a narrow, opaque, technocratic process involving EU officials and domestic civil servants oriented towards relations with European institutions, rather than a broad, transparent process of public deliberation open to all those with a stake in the outcome"* (Sabel/Zeitlin 2008, 316).

But what about in terms of functionality? Are the critics right and is the OMC just a paper tiger? Or is it an effective and necessary instrument of governance in a globalized world, even it is a soft law? The next chapter tries to find answers to these questions.

3. The Evaluation of the Open Method of Coordination

The debate about the effectiveness of the OMC is essentially a debate about the effectiveness of soft law (Trubek/Trubek 2005, 343-344). Therefore, a summary about the pros and cons of the alleged effectiveness of soft law will follow, before starting the evaluation of the OMC.

Trubek and Trubek found six features that could explain why, despite a lack of uniform rules or formal sanctions, soft law might work to bring about change: shaming, diffusion through mimesis or discourse, deliberation, learning, and networks (Trubek/Trubek 2005, 356). Trubek and Trubek write about these features: *"Where shaming, mimesis, and discursive transformation theories focus on how ideas originating at the top and embedded in the guidelines 'diffuse' throughout the EU, alternative accounts stress ways in which the new processes foster experimentation, deliberation, and learning"* (Trubek/Trubek 2005, 358). Further they criticize the exaggerated glorification of hard law and point out that member states also do not often stick to hard law (Trubek/Trubek 2005, 361).

On the con site, critics claim that soft laws are ineffective and even dangerous for European integration (Trubek/Trubek 2005, 344, 351, 355). Especially "euro-corporatist" claim that a Social Europe built upon soft law mechanism could prevent a real European integration into one large European welfare state. (Trubek/Trubek 2005, 352-353).

In terms of the OMC, Buchkremer and Zirra write that it may foster learning but due to a lack of sanctions and a broad scope of interpretation in the benchmarking process, it fall short of expectations (Buchkremer/Zirra 2007, 165). Further they show in their survey about the OMC that vague indicators and a lack of rankings and regards prevent a proper benchmarking (Buchkremer/Zirra 2007, 168-175). After an analysis of the outputs of OMC based decision-making in Italy, France and Germany, Buchkremer and Zirra comes to the conclusion that the OMC is in its present form ineffective (Buchkremer/Zirra 2007, 175, 470).

Sabel and Zeitlin arrive at similar conclusions and emphasize the results of NGOs that were in charged by the European commission to evaluate the OMC (Sabel/Zeitlin 2008, 318). Two of these NGOs are the "European Federation of National Organizations Working with the Homeless" (FEANTSA) and the "European Anti-poverty Network" (EAPN) and their results are here presented:

The FEANTSA writes in its research paper "Evaluation of the Open Method of Coordination in the field of social protection" right at the beginning that a proper evaluation of the OMC is a difficult undertaking (FEANTSA 2007, 2). Trubek, Trubek and Mosher support this statement and refer in their own studies to the difficult evaluability of the OMC, too (Trubek/Trubek 2005, 344 | Trubek/Mosher 2001, 17). Nevertheless, after its analysis FEANTSA came to the same conclusion like Buchkremer and Zirra, that on the one hand the OMC fosters knowledge sharing among the member states (FEANTSA 2007, 6), but on the other a proper benchmarking process is impossible. In conclusion, the critics of the FEANTSA are: Firstly, the OMC focuses too much on procedures and too little on content (FEANTSA 2007, 2). Secondly, indicators and targets have been lacking and could not foster reforms in different member states (FEANTSA 2007, 3). And thirdly, the quality of the consultation varies much from country to country (FEANTSA 2007, 5).

But compared with the results of the EAPN survey, the FEANTSA results became harmless. The EAPN survey could hardly find positive aspects of the OMC and came to a shattering conclusion (EAPN 2008, 3). In their opinion, the ability of the OMC is "toothless" and in every respect to vague (EAPN 2008, 2). EAPNs conclusion is that a soft law like the OMC only can work with "hard targets" and strong formal reports and rankings (EAPN 2008, 3-5).

Although this evaluation of the OMC show that without important improvements the OMC is "toothless" (EAPN 2008, 2), this need not apply for soft law at all. On the contrary, for example evaluations of the EES, the forerunner of the OMC, show that under appropriate circumstances soft law can work very well (Trubek/Mosher 2001, 21-23 | Trubek/Trubek 2005, 349-351 | Sabel/Zeitlin 2008, 291 | Buchkremer/Zirra 2007, 202, 493). Although Trubek and Mosher claim for a better learning process regarding the EES (Trubek/Mosher 2001, 18-19), they also point out the notable effectiveness of the EES (Trubek/Mosher 2001, 21-23). In another survey, Trubek and Trubek underline these positive findings about the EES (Trubek/Trubek 2005, 349-351). Sabel and Zeitlin mainly emphasize the good indicators and proper benchmarking process (Sabel/Zeitlin 2008, 291), while Buchkremer and Zirra commend the mandatory institutionalization of the EES compared to the OMC (Buchkremer/Zirra 2007, 202).

Referring to the research question *"In how far is the OMC an effective tool for European social governance?"* the conclusion is that "soft law may be harder than you think" (Trubek/Trubek 2005, 356), but different scholars and surveys show, that without "hard targets" and a better benchmarking process the OMC fails to foster a more social Europe. In the next chapter policy recommendations will be presented that may improve these problems.

4. Policy Recommendations

In term of socio economic governance, decision-makers in the member states and the EU has to decide whether they want a "euro-corporatist-like" European welfare state built upon hard law (Trubek/Trubek 2005, 352-353), or a decentralized and subsidiary social Europe, where the responsibility remains within the member states. If they choose the last one, soft law could contribute proper mechanism to reach this goal. However, this is only possible if the problems, identified in several surveys and this term paper, would be resolved. Although the following policy recommendation contains only rough suggestions, this does not change their importance.

First of all, the OMC need a further institutionalization. Until now the OMC is grounded on Article 151-153 in the Treaty on the functioning of the European Union, but not mentioned explicitly (Buchkremer/Zirra 2007, 166). This should be changed, if only for reasons of a technocratic democracy deficit (Sabel/Zeitlin 2008, 316). The OMC and the institutions involved in the OMC and their duties should be explicitly mentioned in the treaties.

From a content point of view, even more must be done. Like most scholars agree, the benchmarking process of the OMC need a reformation (Buchkremer/Zirra 2007, 168-175 | Sabel/Zeitlin 2008, 316-318 | Trubek/Trubek 2005, 344 | Trubek/Mosher 2001, 17). The policy recommendations of the EAPN appear here very helpful:

- The EU should setup an OMC webpage, where EU citizens can inform themselves and where the process of member states can be monitored (EAPN 2008, 2).

- The EU should create a Scoreboard linked to a Website display, providing a yearly assessment, highlighting good and bad performance at national level (EAPN 2008, 3).

- The EU should give the OMC "hard targets" based on quantifiable indicators (EAPN 2008, 3).

- The EU should develop indicators of participation and governance at different levels (European, regional and local) which will enable effective benchmarking and continuous evaluation (EAPN 2008, 5).

- The EU should develop an independent structure of local observatories which could provide in recommendations (EAPN 2008, 3).

- The EU should return to annual reporting; short document reviewing progress on identified priorities and targets (EAPN 2008, 4).

- The EU should provide a formal report on outcomes which contains country specific recommendations following Member States' annual reports on the structural funds (EAPN 2008, 6).

5. Bibliography

Armstrong, Kenneth A.. 2010. *Governing Social Inclusion: Europeanization through Policy Coordination.* Oxford: Oxford University Press.

Borrás, Susana/Kerstin Jacobsson. 2004. "The open method of co-ordination and new governance patterns in the EU." *Journal of European Public Policy* 11 (2): 185-208.

Buchkremer, Jenny/Sascha Zirra. 2007. "Die Offene Methode der Koordinierung. Ein Beitrag zur Modernisierung nationaler Sozial und Beschäftigungspolitiken? Abschlussbericht." Deutsche Forschungsgemeinschaft HE 2174/5-1. Bonn: Deutsche Forschungsgemeinschaft.

Consilium.europa.eu. 2000. *Lisbon European Council Presidency Conclusions 2000.* http://alturl.com/jxxii, Accessed on 04.01.2013.

European Anti-poverty Network. 2008. *EAPN Proposals for Strengthening the OMC.* http://alturl.com/rtvpw, Accessed on 05.01.2013.

European Federation of national organizations working with the homeless. 2007. *FEANTSA Evaluation of the Open Method of Coordination in the field of social protection.* http://alturl.com/c9t7r, Accessed on 05.01.2013.

Sabel, Charles F./Jonathan Zeitlin. 2008. "Learning from Difference: The New Architecture of Experimentalist Governance in the EU." *European Law Journal* 14 (3): 271–327.

Süddeutsche.de. 2013. *Arbeitsmarkt - EU: Fast 20 Millionen Arbeitslose in Euro-Zone Mitte 2013.* http://alturl.com/47zqf, Accessed on 04.01.2013.

Trubek, David M./James S. Mosher. 2001. „New Governance, EU Employment Policy, and the European Social Model." Jean Monnet Working Paper No. 6/01. Cambridge, Massachusetts: Harvard Law School.

Trubek, David M./Louise G. Trubek. 2005. "Hard and Soft Law in the Construction of Social Europe: the Role of the Open Method of Co-ordination." *European Law Journal*, 11 (3): 343–364.